W9-BHO-356

ACOUSTIC ROCK HITS
FOR EASY GUITAR

Alfred

ISBN-10: 0-7390-4204-1
ISBN-13: 978-0-7390-4204-5

CONTENTS

ALL THE PRETTY LITTLE PONIES

Words and Music by
KENNY LOGGINS and DAVID PACK

All the Pretty Little Ponies - 3 - 1

4

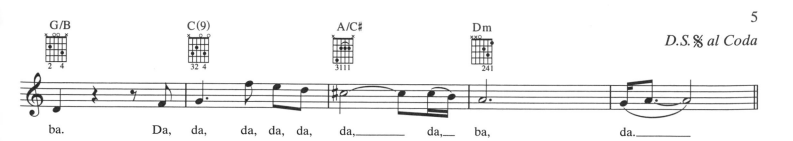

D.S. ℅ al Coda

ba.   Da, da,   da, da, da,   da,_____ da, ba,   da._____

⊕ Coda
Verse 3:
A capella

Hush - a - bye,_____   don't____ you cry.____   Go   to   sleep,_

____ my lit - tle ba - by._____   When   you   wake,_____

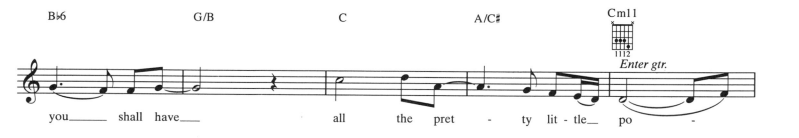

you_____ shall have____   all   the pret - ty lit - tle_ po -

Enter gtr.

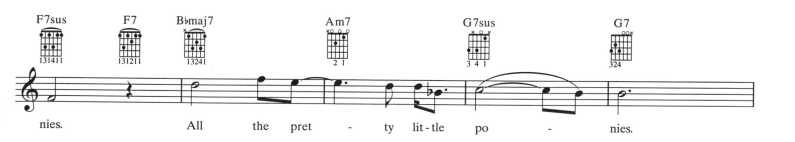

nies.   All   the   pret - ty lit - tle po - nies.

Freely

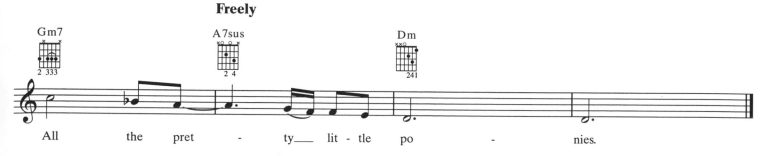

All   the   pret - ty__ lit - tle po - nies.

BOTH SIDES NOW

Words and Music by
JONI MITCHELL

Capo at 2nd fret.

Moderately slow

1. Rows and flows of an-gel hair, and
2.3. *See additional lyrics*

ice cream cas-tles in the air,___ and feath-er can-yons___

___ ev-'ry-where; I've looked at clouds that way.

But now they on-ly block the sun;___ they rain and snow__ on

ev-'ry - one.__ So man-y things I___ would have done,

but clouds got in my way.

1. I've looked at clouds from
2.3. *See additional lyrics*

*Original recording in F♯ major.
**Sung octave lower.

Both Sides Now - 2 - 1

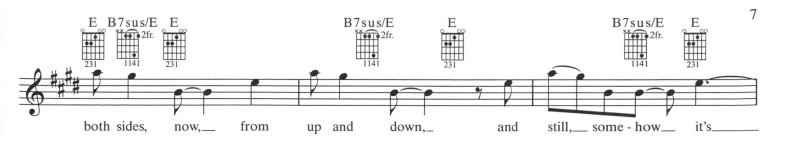

both sides, now,___ from up and down,___ and still,___ some-how___ it's_____

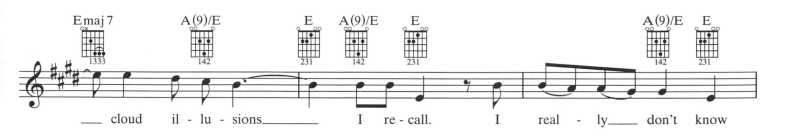

___ cloud il-lu-sions_____ I re-call. I real-ly___ don't know

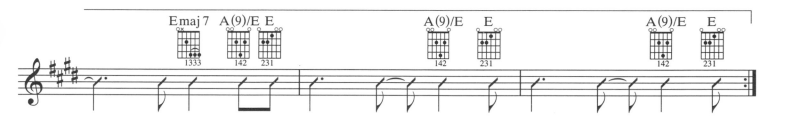

clouds_____ at___ all.

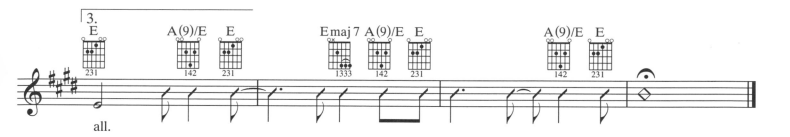

all.

Verse 2:
Moons and Junes and Ferris wheels,
The dizzy dancing way you feel,
As ev'ry fairy tale comes real;
I've looked at love that way.
But now it's just another show;
You leave 'em laughing when you go.
And if you care, don't let them know;
Don't give yourself away.

Chorus 2:
I've looked at love from both sides now,
From give and take, and still somehow
It's love's illusions I recall.
I really don't know love at all.

Verse 3:
Tears and fears and feeling proud,
To say "I love you" right out loud,
Dreams and schemes and circus crowds;
I've looked at life that way.
But now old friends are acting strange;
They shake their heads, they say I've changed.
Well, something's lost but something's gained
In living every day.

Chorus 3:
I've looked at life from both sides now,
From win and lose, and still, somehow
It's life's illusions I recall.
I really don't know life at all.

BIG YELLOW TAXI

Acous. Gtr. in Open E tuning:
⑥ = E ③ = G♯
⑤ = B ② = B
④ = E ① = E

Words and Music by
JONI MITCHELL

Moderately ♩ = 104

Intro:
A 5fr.
B 7fr.
Acous. Gtr.
mf
E
A(9)/E
E
1. They
Verse:
A 5fr.
E
paved par - a - dise, put up a park - ing lot.
2.3.4. See additional lyrics
A 5fr.
B 7fr.
With a pink ho - tel, a bou-tique, and a swing - ing

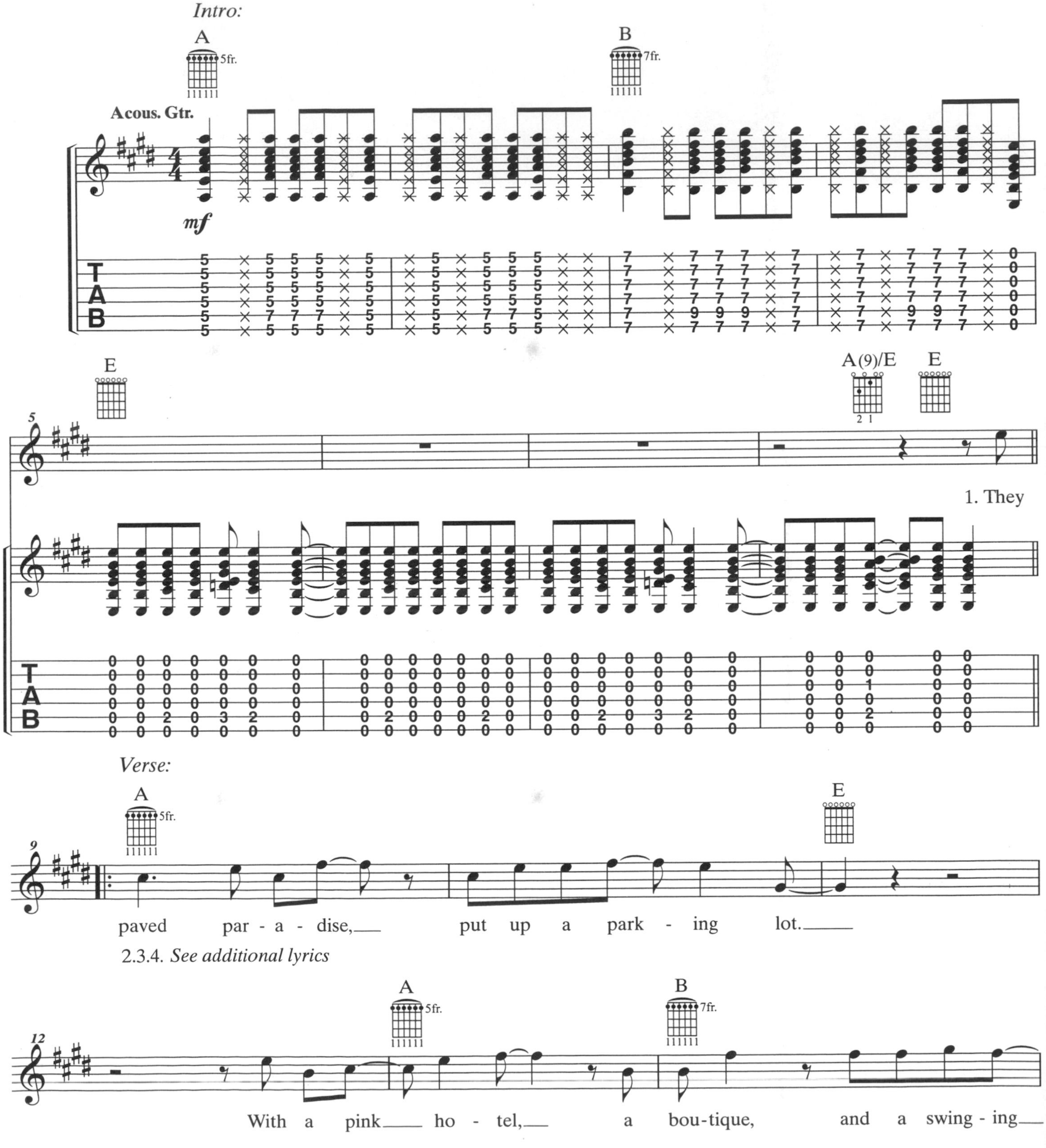

Chorus:

10

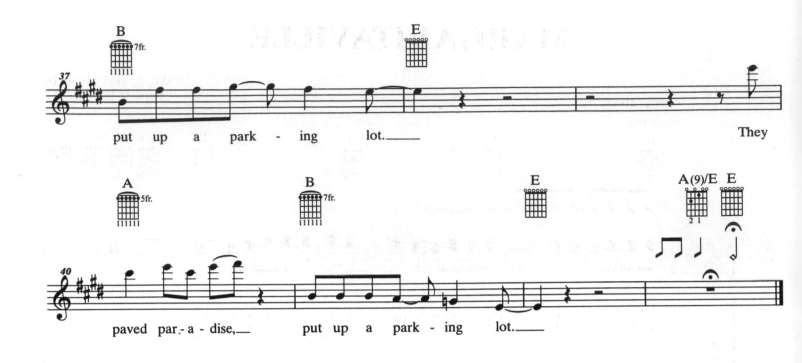

put up a park - ing lot.___ They

paved par - a - dise,___ put up a park - ing lot.___

Verse 2:
They took all the trees,
Put 'em in a tree museum.
And they charged the people
A dollar and a half just to see 'em.
(To Chorus:)

Verse 3:
Hey farmer, farmer,
Put away that DDT now.
Give me spots on my apples
But leave me the birds and the bees,
Please!
(To Chorus:)

Verse 4:
Late last night
I heard the screen door slam.
And a big yellow taxi
Took away my old man.
(To Chorus:)

MARGARITAVILLE

Words and Music by
JIMMY BUFFETT

Margaritaville - 3 - 1

12

D.S. 𝄋 al Coda

Coda

Yes, and some peo-ple claim__ that there's__ a

wom - an to blame_____ and I know__ it's my own__ damn fault.__

Verse 2:
Don't know the reason,
I stayed here all season
With nothing to show but this brand new tattoo.
But it's a real beauty,
A Mexican cutie,
How it got here I haven't a clue.
(To Chorus:)

Verse 4:
I blew out my flip-flop,
Stepped on a pop top;
Cut my heel, had to cruise on back home.
But there's booze in the blender,
And soon it will render
That frozen concoction that helps me hang on.
(To Chorus:)

*Verse 3:
Old men in tank tops
Cruising the gift shops
Checking out the chiquitas down by the shore.
They dream about weight loss,
Wish they could be their own boss.
Those three-day vacations become such a bore.

*"Lost" verse (Live version only)

GOOD RIDDANCE (TIME OF YOUR LIFE)

Lyrics by BILLIE JOE
Music by BILLIE JOE and GREEN DAY

HEART OF GOLD

Words and Music by
NEIL YOUNG

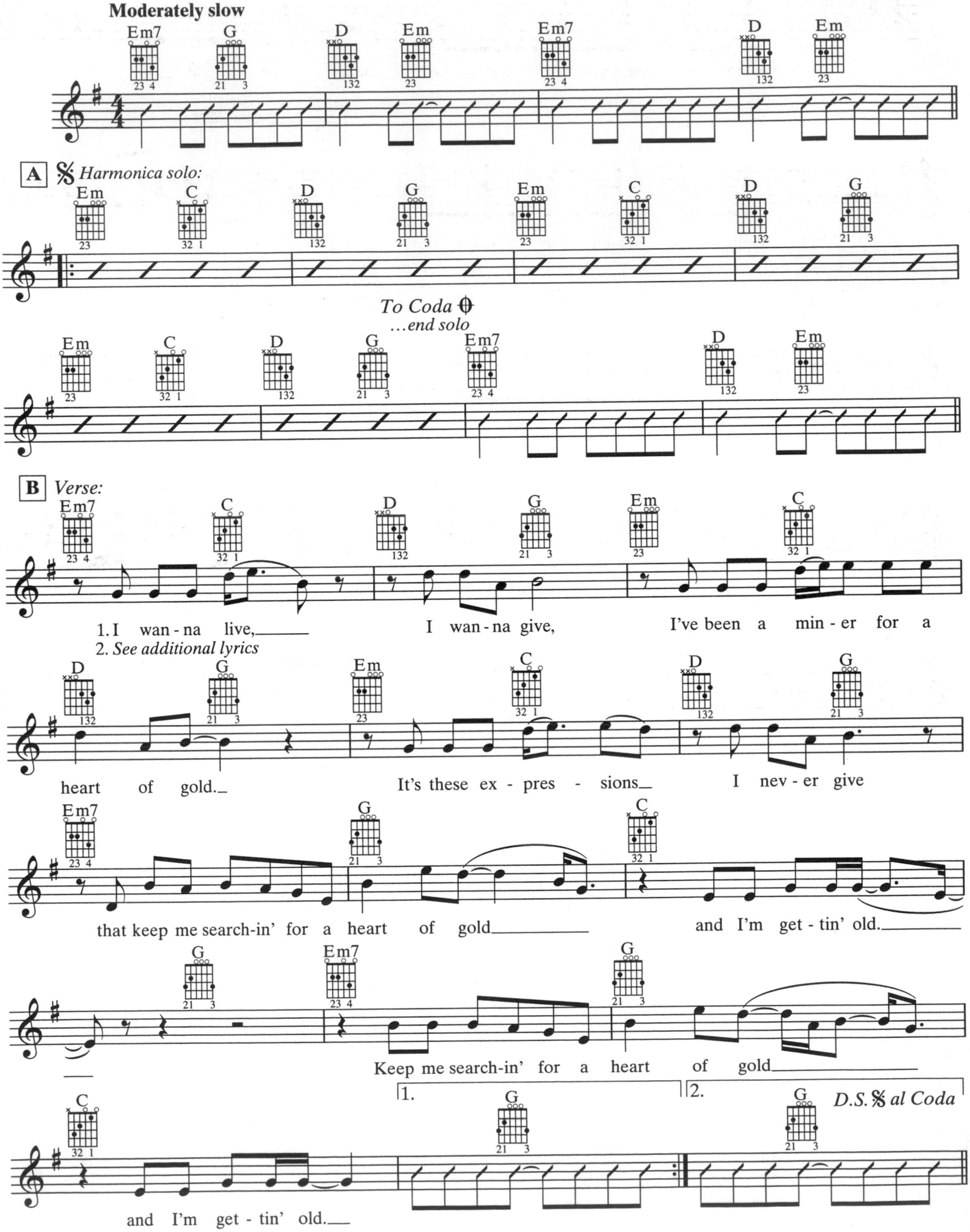

Moderately slow
Em7 G D Em Em7 D Em
A Harmonica solo:
Em C D G Em C D G
To Coda
...end solo
Em C D G Em7 D Em
B Verse:
Em7 C D G Em C
1. I wan-na live, I wan-na give, I've been a min-er for a
2. See additional lyrics
D G Em C D G
heart of gold. It's these ex-pres-sions I nev-er give
Em7 G C
that keep me search-in' for a heart of gold and I'm get-tin' old.
G Em7 G
Keep me search-in' for a heart of gold
C 1. G 2. G D.S. al Coda
and I'm get-tin' old.

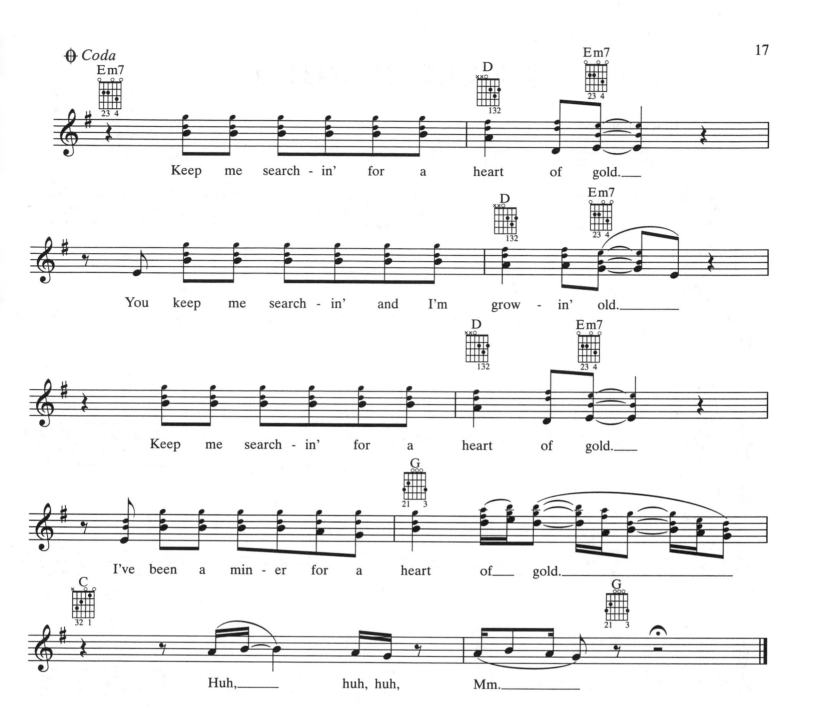

⊕ *Coda*

Keep me search - in' for a heart of gold.___

You keep me search - in' and I'm grow - in' old.___

Keep me search - in' for a heart of gold.___

I've been a min - er for a heart of___ gold.___

Huh,___ huh, huh, Mm.___

Verse 2:
I've been to Hollywood,
I've been to Redwood.
I'd cross the ocean for a heart of gold.
I've been in my mind, it's such a fine line
That keeps me searchin' for a heart of gold
And I'm gettin' old.
Keep me searchin' for a heart of gold
And I'm gettin' old.
(To Harmonica solo:)

OLD MAN

Words and Music by
NEIL YOUNG

Old Man - 2 - 1

Verse 2:
Lullabys look in your eyes,
Run around the same old town,
Doesn't mean that much to me
To mean that much to you.
I've been first and last,
Look at how the time goes past,
But I'm all alone at last,
Rollin' home to you.
(To Chorus:)

PEACEFUL EASY FEELING

Words and Music by
JACK TEMPCHIN

Peaceful Easy Feeling - 2 - 1

Verse 2:
And I found out a long time ago
What a woman can do to your soul.
Ah, but she can't take you anyway,
You don't already know.
(To Chorus:)

Verse 3:
I get this feelin' I may know you
As a lover and a friend.
But this voice keeps whispering in my other ear,
Tells me I may never see you again.
(To Chorus:)

PHOTOGRAPHS & MEMORIES

Words and Music by JIM CROCE

RIPPLE

Words by ROBERT HUNTER
Music by JERRY GARCIA

Moderately
Verse:

1. If my words did glow___ with the gold of sun - shine___
2. It's a hand me down,___ the thoughts are bro - ken,___
3.4. *See additional lyrics*

and my tunes___ were played___ on the harp___ un - strung.___
per - haps___ they're bet - ter left un - sung.___

___ Would you hear my voice___ come through the mu - sic?___
___ I don't know,___ don't real - ly care.

1.3.
Would you hold___ it___ near___ as it were___your own?.___
Let there be songs.

to fill___ the air.___

Chorus:

Rip - ple in___ still___ wa - ter,___ when there is___

25

Verse 3:
Reach out your hand,
If your cup be empty.
If your cup is full,
May it be again.
Let it be known,
There is a fountain
That was not made
By the hands of men.

Verse 4:
There is a road,
No simple highway,
Between the dawn,
And the dark of night.
And if you go,
No one may follow,
That path is for
Your steps alone.
(To Chorus:)

SISTER GOLDEN HAIR

Words and Music by
GERRY BECKLEY

SUNSHINE ON MY SHOULDERS

Words by
JOHN DENVER
Music by
JOHN DENVER, MIKE TAYLOR and DICK KNISS

Moderately slow ♩ = 74

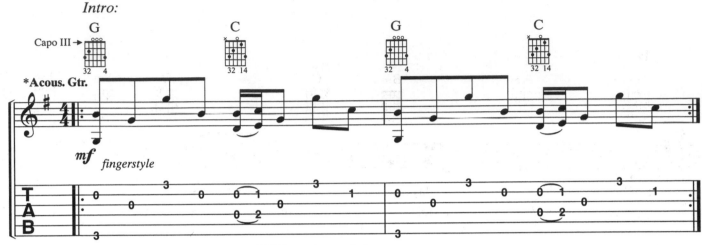

*Acous. Gtr. w/capo III. Chord frames and TAB numbers relative to capo.
Recording sounds 1 1/2 steps higher than written.

Sun-shine on my shoul-ders___ makes me hap-py.___

Sun-shine in my eyes___ can make my cry.___

Sun-shine on the wa-ter looks so love-ly.___

30

Chorus:

Sun - shine on my shoul - ders____ makes me hap - py.____

Sun - shine in my eyes____ can make my cry._____

Sun - shine on the wa - ter looks so love - ly._____

Sun - shine almost al - ways_____ makes me high._____

Sun - shine al-most all____ the time____ makes me____ high._____

Sun - shine al-most al - ways..._____

TAKE IT EASY

Words and Music by JACKSON BROWNE
and GLENN FREY

Moderately ♩ = 138

Intro:

1. Well, I'm a

32

Take It Easy - 5 - 3

D.S. % al Coda

3. Well, I'm a

Coda

Come on,___ ba - by, don't say___ may-

-be. I___ got - ta know if your___ sweet

love___ is gon - na save_____ me.___

Outro:

Ooh,_____ ooh,_____ ooh,_____ ooh._____

Ooh,_____ ooh,_____ ooh,_____ ooh._____

Ooh,_____ Oh,__ we got it eas - y.

(Ooh._____)

We ought-ta take it eas - y.

y.

Verse 2:
Well, I'm a standin' on a corner in Winslow, Arizona,
And such a fine sight to see:
It's a girl, my Lord, in a flat bed Ford
Slowin' down to take a look at me.

Verse 3:
Well, I'm a runnin' down the road, tryin' to loosen my load,
Got a world of trouble on my mind.
Lookin' for a lover who won't blow my cover,
She's so hard to find.
(To Chorus:)

Chorus 2:
Come on, baby, don't say maybe.
I gotta know if your sweet love is gonna save me.
We may lose and we may win, though we will never be here again.
So open up, I'm climbin' in, so take it easy.
(To Guitar Solo:)

TIN MAN

Words and Music by
DEWEY BUNNELL

TAKE ME HOME, COUNTRY ROADS

Words and Music by
JOHN DENVER, BILL DANOFF
and TAFFY NIVERT

Take Me Home, Country Roads - 3 - 1

VENTURA HIGHWAY

Words and Music by
DEWEY BUNNELL

Moderately fast ♩ = 130
Intro:

Ventura Highway - 3 - 1

your hair___ and the days sur - round_ your day - light there.___ Sea - sons cry - ing, no___

___ de - spair,___ al - li - ga - tor liz - ards in___ the air,_____ in the air._____

___ Did di di di di dit di di di di di dit, Did di di di di dit di di di di di dit,

Did di di di di dit di di di di di dit, Did di di di di dit di di di di di dit,

1. D.S. 𝄋 **2.** *Repeat and fade*

Did di di di di dit di di di di di dit, Did di di di di dit di di di di di dit. Did di di di di dit di di di di di dit.

Verse 2:
Wishin' on a falling star,
Watchin' for the early train.
Sorry, boy, but I've been hit by purple rain.
Aw, come on, Joe,
You can always change your name.
Thanks, a lot, son, just the same.
(To Chorus:)

WAKE ME UP WHEN SEPTEMBER ENDS

Moderately ♩ = 104

Words by BILLIE JOE
Music by GREEN DAY

GUITAR TAB GLOSSARY **

TABLATURE EXPLANATION

READING TABLATURE: Tablature illustrates the six strings of the guitar. Notes and chords are indicated by the placement of fret numbers on a given string(s).

String ⑥, 3rd Fret   String ① 12th Fret   A "C" Chord   C Chord Arpeggiated
String ③ 13th Fret

BENDING NOTES

HALF STEP: Play the note and bend string one half step.*

WHOLE STEP: Play the note and bend string one whole step.

WHOLE STEP AND A HALF: Play the note and bend string a whole step and a half.

SLIGHT BEND (Microtone): Play the note and bend string slightly to the equivalent of half a fret.

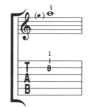

PREBEND (Ghost Bend): Bend to the specified note, before the string is picked.

PREBEND AND RELEASE: Bend the string, play it, then release to the original note.

REVERSE BEND: Play the already-bent string, then immediately drop it down to the fretted note.

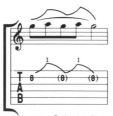

BEND AND RELEASE: Play the note and gradually bend to the next pitch, then release to the original note. Only the first note is attacked.

UNISON BEND: Play both notes and immediately bend the lower note to the same pitch as the higher note.

DOUBLE NOTE BEND: Play both notes and immediately bend both strings simultaneously.

BENDS INVOLVING MORE THAN ONE STRING: Play the note and bend string while playing an additional note (or notes) on another string(s). Upon release, relieve pressure from additional note(s), causing original note to sound alone.

BENDS INVOLVING STATIONARY NOTES: Play notes and bend lower pitch, then hold until release begins (indicated at the point where line becomes solid).

TREMOLO BAR

SPECIFIED INTERVAL: The pitch of a note or chord is lowered to a specified interval and then may or may not return to the original pitch. The activity of the tremolo bar is graphically represented by peaks and valleys.

UN-SPECIFIED INTERVAL: The pitch of a note or a chord is lowered to an unspecified interval.

HARMONICS

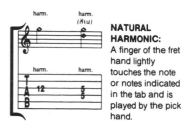

NATURAL HARMONIC: A finger of the fret hand lightly touches the note or notes indicated in the tab and is played by the pick hand.

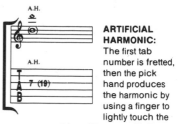

ARTIFICIAL HARMONIC: The first tab number is fretted, then the pick hand produces the harmonic by using a finger to lightly touch the same string at the second tab number (in parenthesis) and is then picked by another finger.

ARTIFICIAL "PINCH" HAR-MONIC: A note is fretted as indicated by the tab, then the pick hand produces the harmonic by squeezing the pick firmly while using the tip of the index finger in the pick attack. If parenthesis are found around the fretted note, it does not sound. No parenthesis means both the fretted note and A.H. are heard simultaneously.

*A half step is the smallest interval in Western music; it is equal to one fret. A whole step equals two frets.

**By Kenn Chipkin and Aaron Stang

RHYTHM SLASHES

STRUM INDICATIONS: Strum with indicated rhythm.

The chord voicings are found on the first page of the transcription underneath the song title.

INDICATING SINGLE NOTES USING RHYTHM SLASHES: Very often single notes are incorporated into a rhythm part. The note name is indicated above the rhythm slash with a fret number and a string indication.

ARTICULATIONS

HAMMER ON: Play lower note, then "hammer on" to higher note with another finger. Only the first note is attacked.

LEFT HAND HAMMER: Hammer on the first note played on each string with the left hand.

PULL OFF: Play higher note, then "pull off" to lower note with another finger. Only the first note is attacked.

FRET-BOARD TAPPING: "Tap" onto the note indicated by + with a finger of the pick hand, then pull off to the following note held by the fret hand.

TAP SLIDE: Same as fretboard tapping, but the tapped note is slid randomly up the fretboard, then pulled off to the following note.

BEND AND TAP TECHNIQUE: Play note and bend to specified interval. While holding bend, tap onto note indicated.

LEGATO SLIDE: Play note and slide to the following note. (Only first note is attacked).

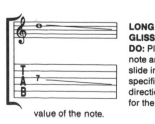

LONG GLISSANDO: Play note and slide in specified direction for the full value of the note.

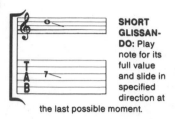

SHORT GLISSANDO: Play note for its full value and slide in specified direction at the last possible moment.

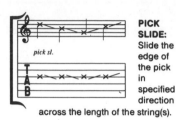

PICK SLIDE: Slide the edge of the pick in specified direction across the length of the string(s).

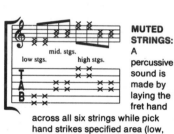

MUTED STRINGS: A percussive sound is made by laying the fret hand across all six strings while pick hand strikes specified area (low, mid, high strings).

PALM MUTE: The note or notes are muted by the palm of the pick hand by lightly touching the string(s) near the bridge.

TREMOLO PICKING: The note or notes are picked as fast as possible.

TRILL: Hammer on and pull off consecutively and as fast as possible between the original note and the grace note.

ACCENT: Notes or chords are to be played with added emphasis.

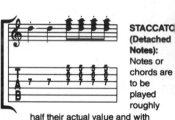

STACCATO (Detached Notes): Notes or chords are to be played roughly half their actual value and with separation.

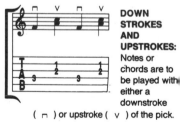

DOWN STROKES AND UPSTROKES: Notes or chords are to be played with either a downstroke (⊓) or upstroke (∨) of the pick.

VIBRATO: The pitch of a note is varied by a rapid shaking of the fret hand finger, wrist, and forearm.